A Call to Christians

8

The Single Sermon Series

A Call to Christians

Chris Reed

Publishing
Angel
Climbing

A Call to Christians
Written by Chris Reed

Edited by Lisa Soland
Text copyright © 2024 Chris Reed

Published in 2024 by:
Climbing Angel Publishing
PO Box 32381
Knoxville, Tennessee 37930
http://www.ClimbingAngel.com

First Edition: August 2024
Printed in the United States of America

Graphic Design: Climbing Angel Publishing

ISBN: 978-1-956218-39-8
Library of Congress Control Number: 2024915208

This book is dedicated to my wife, Lindsey,
who is the very embodiment of a loving wife
and mother. God sure knew what he was
doing when He brought us together.
I love you.

James 4:1-12

What causes quarrels and what causes fights among you? Is it not this, that your passions are at war within you? 2 You desire and do not have, so you murder. You covet and cannot obtain, so you fight and quarrel. You do not have, because you do not ask. 3 You ask and do not receive, because you ask wrongly, to spend it on your passions.4 You adulterous people! Do you not know that friendship with the world is enmity with God? Therefore whoever wishes to be a friend of the world makes himself an enemy of God.5 Or do you suppose it is to no purpose that the Scripture says, "He yearns jealously over the spirit that he has made to dwell in us"?6 But he gives more grace. Therefore it says, "God opposes the proud but gives grace to the humble." 7 Submit yourselves therefore to God. Resist the devil, and he will flee from you. 8 Draw near to God, and he will draw near to you. Cleanse your hands, you sinners, and purify your hearts, you double-minded.9 Be wretched and mourn and weep. Let your laughter be turned to mourning and your joy to gloom. 10 Humble yourselves before the Lord, and he will exalt you. 11 Do not speak evil against one another, brothers. The one who speaks against a brother or judges his brother, speaks evil against the law and judges the law. But if you judge the law, you are not a doer of the law but a judge. 12 There is only one lawgiver and judge, he who is able to save and to destroy. But who are you to judge your neighbor?

A Call to Christians

When examining the difference between God's wisdom and the world's wisdom, we see a contrast in our outward actions and our underlying motivations.

At the end of his third chapter, James tells us that the world's wisdom is rooted in bitter jealousy and selfish ambition, resulting in disorder in every vile action. However, God's wisdom is pure, peaceable, gentle, reasonable, full of mercy, impartial, and sincere, resulting in good fruits. Good ends do not justify evil means. God wants pure and holy outward actions motivated by pure and holy inward hearts. These actions are at the core of what it means to be Christ's disciples amid a worldly culture.

James' audience in the first century A.D. struggled with many of the same conflicts we struggle with today in our church and within ourselves. Increasingly, our religious beliefs and the society in which we live are coming into conflict. The "moral norms" we grew up with and hold dear are no longer "normal." They are no longer "norms" at all.

As a middle school teacher, I witnessed this difference in behavior firsthand. If you want to know about society and human nature, be a middle school teacher. Middle school children are poorly filtered microcosms of our society.

I had many great experiences, much more than bad, for sure. I taught a lot of great kids, but one of the things I took away from that experience was how normal and acceptable it is now for people to lie.

When I was growing up, my parents didn't like it when they caught me lying. The degree of punishment I received taught me that lying was not okay. So, I grew up holding this as a norm and believed that everyone thought this way. Yes, people lie, but maybe they ought to at least think badly of it. Well, I learned in middle school that this was not the case.

I was amazed at how quick and natural the response to lie was. The children didn't think twice about it. Whenever I would confront them with one of their inappropriate actions, I was surprised at how quickly they would lie about it, even if they knew I had just watched them commit the action. The lie remained automatic, even when they did nothing wrong. Telling the truth would have been an acceptable answer and would not have resulted in punishment. But still, the lie was the first instinct. And I thought, "How can this be?"

My friend and fellow pastor at West Park, James Lynch, said in a recent sermon, "No lie is little, and no lie is white; they're all big, and they're all dirty."

In our culture, other pillars of society are also eroding. Principles we once took for granted are being tossed out. The traditional family model is breaking down. The institution of marriage is being undermined. Even the existence of truth itself is questioned.

Not long ago, I watched a YouTube video of an interview with a woman arguing over the truth of 2 + 2 = 4. I kid you not. She claimed that "2 + 2 = 4" is oppressive. She said that truth, such as this, should be relative to each individual's experience. It blew my mind. How do we, as Christians, hold to biblical absolutes while living in a culture such as this? Let's face it: America is in the process of being de-churched, and the church is in gradual decline.

THINGS WE'VE TRIED

The critical question is, "How do we as Christians respond to the culture regarding truth in an increasingly secular world?" As individuals and as the church as a whole, we typically respond in one of three ways:

COMPROMISE

As a church, we have compromised the message. We reinterpret verses so they are less offensive and more inclusive. We pick and choose which parts of the Bible are important —which we need to hold on to and which we can let go of. This response to compromising with today's culture is a slippery slope that leads to more compromise. Eventually, you're not compromising anymore because you've abandoned the faith altogether.

As individuals, we've avoided the Bible's approach to resolving conflict and claim ignorance regarding the difficult biblical topics that arise in ordinary conversation. When the Bible presents us with difficult truths, we sometimes let our own opinions shape how we read the scripture instead of letting scripture shape our beliefs, as it should. Responding through compromise doesn't work.

2

ISOLATION

The other way we have responded to conflict is by isolating ourselves. We try to keep the world out. We build a wall around our church and show partiality and favoritism to the kind of people we want to include. We judge and shun people who think differently than we do. We do good, but only to those on the inside, while staying as far away from the mess of our communities and our culture as we can.

As individuals, we hide ourselves and our families under the guise of "protection." And I get that. As a father, I have a God-given duty and responsibility to protect my family and children. But let me tell you a story of where that goes wrong. I was serving at a church and doing a student outreach ministry, reaching out to a rough part of the city. For one week, we went into the community and did outreach. We taught and played games, and then we'd return. But one of the dads wouldn't let his child participate. So the youth pastor talked with the dad, and the father said, "I didn't work this hard just to have my kid go there." Imagine if God the Father had this attitude when He sent His Son to earth. Imagine if Jesus had stayed away from the "hard" places.

Isolation has not worked. Separating ourselves from the culture, as individuals and as the church, has not been a successful response.

3

HATEFUL OPPOSITION

The other way we have responded to the culture is through hateful opposition. As a church, we've made more of a name for ourselves based on what and who we hate rather than what and who we love. This doesn't mean we should love how the world wants us to love. I'm not talking about that. They want us to love by accepting and approving all actions, by seeing every path as equally valid and good. But that's not really love. We are to love the way *God* calls us to love.

Perhaps you've heard the saying that living as Christians and sharing the gospel is like one beggar telling another beggar where to find bread. That is loving. That is love. When we see other beggars heading the wrong way and know that way is empty and full of starvation and hardship and will not get them to where they need to be, what's the loving thing to do? Approve that direction? Accept it? No. The loving thing to do would be to tell them the truth in love. The loving thing to do would be to bring them along, drag them if we must, to where the true bread of life exists.

Instead, we become known for what we oppose. As individuals, we harbor bitterness and anger toward those who have different worldviews than we do. Many times, they're being used by the enemy. Let's remember that our true enemy is not flesh and blood. The true enemy is *using* flesh and blood.

To oppose them, we sometimes lash out with our attitudes or our words. We have become skilled at logging onto social media and firing jabs and hooks through typed words expressing hate rather than truth in love.

These three ways of responding have not worked out well and have led the church in America to a difficult position. We haven't done well with conflict, whether within or without the church, but that's nothing new. Conflict is part of everyone's daily life.

SOURCES OF CONFLICT

In James 4:1-6, the author explains that everyone will have conflict, especially Christians. Christians are going to have conflict in a secular world. Jesus warned us about this. The difference, though, is that Christians have a hope of victory.

Let's read as James describes this conflict in the first six verses of Chapter 4.

What causes quarrels and what causes fights among you? Is it not this, that your

passions are at war within you? You desire and do not have, so you murder. You covet and cannot obtain, so you fight and quarrel. You do not have, because you do not ask. You ask and do not receive, because you ask wrongly, to spend it on your passions. You adulterous people! Do you not know that friendship with the world is enmity with God? Therefore whoever wishes to be a friend of the world makes himself an enemy of God. Or do you suppose it is to no purpose that the Scripture says, "He yearns jealously over the spirit that he has made to dwell in us"? But he gives more grace. Therefore it says, "God opposes the proud but gives grace to the humble."
(James 4:1-6)

The early Christians were facing much of the same conflicts we are today. They were coming into conflict with their culture and each other, which led to fights and arguments. But the quarreling was just a symptom of the problem. The problem at the root of the conflict was something much deeper, ultimately leading to compromise, hypocrisy, and heresy in the worst cases. We want to avoid falling into the same trap. May it not be said of us that we are part of an adulterous generation or that we are the reason for it. As

Christians, we are called to be seriously different.

The first six verses of James, Chapter 4, show us what actions and attitudes cause the problem. The second half (verses 7 to 12) tells us how to avoid and fix the problem. Let's examine the sources of the conflict first.

1

PASSIONS AT WAR

James calls the source of the conflict out right at the beginning—"passions are at war within you." What does James mean by "passions?" In our understanding of the English language, how we use "passions" can be good or bad. Being a passionate person can sometimes be a favorable quality. So, the word here is *Hedone* in the Greek. It is the root of the English word "hedonism" and refers to worldly pleasures, desires, or lusts, as other versions of the Bible translate.

These are not the good kinds of passions. It is these passions that are at war within us. This is the same inner conflict that Paul referred to when he confessed that he knew what he should do but didn't. And he knew the things he shouldn't do, but he did.

For I do not understand my own actions.
For I do not do what I want, but I do
the very thing I hate.
(Romans 7:15)

This is precisely what Paul was getting at in his letter. We must continue fighting this inward battle as long as we are in this world. And by God's grace, we can win.

2

ENVY, JEALOUSY, and PRIDE

The second source of conflict—envy, jealousy, and pride, returns us to the Garden of Eden. How many wars throughout history can be traced back to envy, jealousy, and pride? We want what we don't have; we don't have because we're too prideful to ask God. Even when we do ask, we don't receive because our wills are not aligned with God's will. It sounds a little bit like, *"God told me not to eat the fruit, but if I do, I'll be like God. That sounds good. I want what I don't have. I'll be like God. I'll know what God knows, so I'll eat the fruit."*

Ultimately, pride is at the root of all human sin. The idea that our will is somehow preferable to God's is thoroughly misaligned thinking.

3

COMPROMISE

The third source of conflict is *compromise*. As Christians, we are in the world, but we shouldn't become friends with it. As much as we may want to, the Bible leads us otherwise.

> *"No one can serve two masters, for either he will hate the one and love the other, or he will be devoted to the one and despise the other. You cannot serve God and money."*
> (Matthew 6:24)

Some of these early Christians tried to have friendship with God and friendship with the world, but that can't be done. We can't have it both ways. The Bible says there is a broad path and a narrow path. There is no "slightly narrow" or "slightly broad" path running down the middle.

Our temptation to sin starts with something small. The path diverges, and the worldly path and narrow Godly path separate over something seemingly insignificant at some point along the way. The paths don't seem that far apart to us, so guess what we do? We keep one foot on the Godly path and the other on the worldly path. We think we can walk both! And that works fine for a time (as long as the two stay close together).

But the two paths do not stay close together. They get further and further apart. So, continuing on both paths becomes uncomfortable. We might even try jumping from one to the other, depending upon where we are—in church or at work. You can jump paths. But, even then, after a while, the paths become so far apart that you can't make that jump. Eventually, without God's intervention, we will find ourselves on the broad path.

The root of our conflict is our sinful passions at war within us—our fleshly envy, jealousy, and pride. And then there's our idea that we can somehow have it both ways, which also comes from our pride.

JAMES' CALL TO CHRISTIANS

In James 4:7-10, our author switches gears and shows us how not to be this way. He describes the problem he set out at the end of Chapter 3, pitting Godly and worldly wisdom against each other. In James 4:6, he shows us how badly we've handled that conflict, and now, in verses 7-10, he tells us what to do about it.

Submit yourselves therefore to God. Resist the devil, and he will flee from you. Draw near to God, and he will draw near to you. Cleanse your

hands, you sinners, and purify your hearts, you
double-minded. Be wretched and mourn and
weep. Let your laughter be turned to mourning
and your joy to gloom. Humble yourselves before
the Lord, and he will exalt you.
(James 4:7-10)

SUBMIT TO GOD

First, James says to submit to God. This is the
first step in salvation and the first step of
every day since your salvation. Picking up your
cross daily and following Jesus begins with
submitting your own will to the will of God.
Every day, we must consciously put God above
ourselves.

But seek first the kingdom of God and his
righteousness, and all these things
will be added to you.
(Matthew 6:33)

This Bible verse clearly states that we are
to seek God's kingdom first. In Matthew 6:33,
Jesus solves one of the conflicts James has
mentioned by instructing that God will give us
all these things if we seek Him first. We don't
have to be jealous or envious because our Lord

will provide for us. But first, we must submit to Him.

2

RESIST THE DEVIL

Secondly, we are to resist the devil. Easier said than done, right? The devil can read the Bible and knew the truth about "warring passions within us" long before James wrote it down. Satan knows what's going on. He knows our passions are at war within us, and he knows which ones to use to tempt us. He is watchful. So, resisting the devil is hard.

We must look to Jesus and His example of successfully resisting the devil in the wilderness. Though Jesus was tired, hungry, and worn out, He resisted the devil using Scripture. However, his resistance was more than simply quoting verses from the Old Testament. What was more significant than Jesus memorizing and quoting Scripture was that He knew the heart and mind of God. He knew what the devil was trying to do. He was trying to subvert God's Will, and because Jesus knew God and His will, He knew exactly how to use those verses to resist the evil one. And the devil fled.

DRAW NEAR TO GOD

In verse 8, James says, "Draw near to God, and He will draw near to you." Nowhere is this verse more effectively illustrated than in John 15. Jesus' words present a beautiful picture of what it means to draw near to God.

I am the vine; you are the branches. Whoever abides in me and I in him, he it is that bears much fruit, for apart from me you can do nothing. If anyone does not abide in me he is thrown away like a branch and withers; and the branches are gathered, thrown into the fire, and burned. If you abide in me, and my words abide in you, ask whatever you wish, and it will be done for you.
(John 15:5-7)

By this my Father is glorified, that you bear much fruit and so prove to be my disciples. As the Father has loved me, so have I loved you. Abide in my love.
(John 15:8-9)

The troubles we are facing, as described by James in this chapter, have already been addressed by Jesus. We quarrel, we don't have, we don't ask, and we ask wrongly because we don't abide. If we draw near to

Him and abide in Him and His words in us,
we will ask, and God will answer.

4

HUMBLY REPENT

The last thing James challenges us to do, and
possibly the most difficult of the four, is to
humbly repent our sins. But James doesn't say
it as nicely as that.

> *Cleanse your hands, you sinners, and purify*
> *your hearts, you double-minded. Be wretched*
> *and mourn and weep. Let your laughter be*
> *turned to mourning and your joy to gloom.*
> *Humble yourselves before the Lord,*
> *and he will exalt you.*
> (James 4:8-10)

In humility, we need to repent of our sins.
James is very descriptive here with his
language. He is asking for a true turn from sin,
a true change of heart. James is not saying
that we should walk around with our heads
down and our shoulders hunched in a posture
of defeat because we're taking on the entire
guilt of our sin at all times. Because of other
biblical texts, we know that's not what
Christian life is about. The Christian life is not
about defeat but victory!

So, James is not telling us to go around with our heads down, always contemplating our guilt. He is telling us to turn. And in that, yes, our sin should affect us. We should feel its weight, its wrongness, and the guilt that comes from sinning. But as Christians, this awareness should drive us toward God, not away from Him.

I struggled with this through high school and college, when I would fail. I would fall into a sin, and when I came to the end of it and realized that what I did was wrong, I would ask for forgiveness. Then, for about a week, I would go on hiatus from my relationship with God and try to do everything correctly under my own power. I would try to make myself better and more acceptable to God. Only then could I consider myself worthy to go before Him and start my prayer life and devotions again.

That's not the way to do it. This approach to repentance needs to be corrected. I was wrong. As Christians, when we sin, yes, we should feel sorrowful. We should feel frustrated, even angry sometimes, but these feelings should drive us straight into the arms of the Father because in Him is life. In Him is true forgiveness. When it comes to sin, we should not be like the world which revels in its sin. We should not be like Adam or myself and try to run and hide from our sins. True repentance will balance both sorrow and joy.

Strangely, joy comes from repentance and sorrow from our failure. But even in repentance, joy comes from our hope in Christ and our thankfulness for God's forgiveness and love.

As we read verses 7 through 10, it all seems impossible. James has mapped out an impossible list of dos for us. It is impossible to do this on our own. We need help.

And look how James paints his audience —an adulterous generation. Most assuredly, it's impossible for *them*. Then, in verse seven, James gives them that list. Are you kidding?! They're already in such a mess, quarreling and fighting. How do you expect them to resist the devil on their own? How do you expect them to submit to God? To come to a proper repentance on their own? The good thing is James doesn't expect that. This may be why some people who try Christianity give up. They are like the seeds the sower planted, which grew quickly but were soon choked out. I think some people get fed up with Christianity fast because they don't understand it rightly. They see the Christian faith as an impossible list of dos and don'ts.

And to make matters worse, they get judged. As James points out in verses 11 and 12, some in the church judge when you don't live up to this impossible list. James tells us we are not the judge; only God is.

THE SOLUTION

So, what's the key to living righteously in conflict with a secular world? Grace. Grace is the key.

But he gives more grace. Therefore it says, "God opposes the proud but gives grace to the humble."
(James 4:6)

James knew that grace was the answer all along. He shows us the reasons and the results of following worldly wisdom. He knows that we are hopelessly stuck on our own. This is why he gives us the key in verse 6 before telling us what to do in verses 7-12. "But He gives more grace." James can only call on Christians to do these seemingly impossible things because he knows God's grace is more than enough.

If we are to have any hope, as a church and as Christians individually, we must look to God and fervently ask for His grace.

The Bible says humanity has two possible choices: friend of God or friend of the world. James says to be a friend or follower of the world is to make yourself an enemy of God. Not that God has made you His enemy. You make yourself His enemy. Even then, He will freely give forgiveness and salvation to those who would but ask.

> *...if you confess with your mouth that Jesus is Lord and believe in your heart that God raised him from the dead, you will be saved. For with the heart one believes and is justified, and with the mouth one confesses and is saved. For the Scripture says, "Everyone who believes in him will not be put to shame."*
> (Romans 10:9-11)

So, for the unbeliever today, I challenge you to call on God. Call on His grace and mercy. Believe, repent, and confess, and He will give you His grace and salvation.

For Christians, I challenge you to heed James' words. Pray and identify the worldly desires at work within yourself. Repent and ask God for His grace because we need it. As Christians, we need His grace every single day. If we are to have hope and a chance to answer the call and live seriously differently in this world, we need His grace. If we live differently, things will go well for us in our relationship with God, and the world will see the truth of God's Word through our words and actions.

PRAYER

Thank you for the Word today, Lord. Thank you for being so challenging. As we come into conflict with ourselves, each other, and our world, we pray that You will guide our hearts and minds. We pray that You will give us grace and help us to quell our pride, be humble, and submit our desires to You. Lord, allow us to shine Your light in the world, a world that is increasingly in conflict with us and does not understand You or why we as believers live the way we live or say the things we say. Please give us the strength and courage to answer the call and live differently in this world. It is in Your name that we pray.

ABOUT
CLIMBING ANGEL PUBLISHING

Climbing Angel Publishing shares stories of hope and encouragement, aids in the gathering together of community, and supports the process of betterment. The following books are available at your leading online bookstores.

ADULT BOOKS: (Romans 8:28-30)

In His Image by Sam Polson
(English, Romanian, & Mandarin)
By Faith by Sam Polson (English & Romanian)
My Birthday Gift to Jesus by Lisa Soland
Without Ceasing by Dr. Dennis Davidson
SonLight: Daily Light from the Pages of God's Word
by Sam Polson
Corona Victus: Conquering the Virus of Fear
by Sam Polson (English & Romanian)
*Art Bushing: His Diary, Letters, & Photographs of
WWII* by Art Bushing
*Art & Dotty: His Diary, Their Letters & Photographs of
WWII* by Art Bushing
Trimisul by Stan Johnson (Romanian)
Life Changing Prayer by Sam Polson
The Climbing Angel Christmas Treasury,
variety of authors
J. Calvin Coolidge: Letters from the Korean War
by J. Calvin Coolidge
*Stories from Kingman, AZ: The Heart of Historic Route
66* by Loren B. Wilson
*Pathways: Ancient Paths from the Pages of the Old
Testament* by Sam Polson

THE SINGLE SERMON SERIES: (1 Pet. 3:15)

Jesus is Alive! by Mike Sager
My Mother's Bible by Sam Polson
The Lost Boys by Jake Bishop
Melchizedek: A Shadow of Christ by Jerry Scheumann
A Servant of Christ by James Alan Lynch
Dreaming God's Dream by Dr. Al Cage
Resisting Sin by Colin Hughes
A Call to Christians by Chris Reed

CHILDREN'S BOOKS: (Philippians 4:8)

The Christmas Tree Angel by Lisa Soland
The Unmade Moose by Lisa Soland
Thump by Lisa Soland
Somebunny To Love by Lisa Soland
(English & Mandarin)
The Truth About God's Rainbow by Lisa Soland
God's Promises by Lisa Soland
The Boy & The Bagel Necklace by Lisa Soland
God's Hands and Feet by Lisa Soland
I Like To Be Quiet by Joni Caldwell
Wheels Off! by Karlie Saumier
Ella's Trip of a Lifetime by Melanie Ewbank
Because You Are Mine by Gayle Childress Greene
Jeremy Plays the Blues by Amy Oden Simpson
Bad Hair Day by Jasmyne Simpkins
I Like To Read by Joni Caldwell
Trunks Up! by Karlie Saumier
Perusha's Paradise by Bette Reed Smith
Ruby and the Treasure Within
by Tonya Celeste Hobbs
Abby, the Wonder Dog & her Warrior Princess
by Melanie Ewbank
The Christmas Coat by Lisa Soland
Danger Around the Bend by Karlie Saumier

www.ingramcontent.com/pod-product-compliance
Lightning Source LLC
Chambersburg PA
CBHW051604120626
46551CB00013B/1665